BUILDING BLOCKS OF GEOGRAPHY

ATMOSPHERE AND WEATHER

Written by Alex Woolf

Illustrated by Steve Evans

WORLD BOOK

a Scott Fetzer company
Chicago

World Book, Inc.
180 North LaSalle Street
Suite 900
Chicago, Illinois 60601
USA

For information about other World Book publications,
visit our website at **www.worldbook.com**
or call **1-800-WORLDBK (967-5325).**
For information about sales to schools and libraries,
call 1-800-975-3250 (United States),
or 1-800-837-5365 (Canada).

Library of Congress Cataloging-in-Publication Data
for this volume has been applied for.

Building Blocks of Geography
ISBN: 978-0-7166-4275-6 (set, hc.)

Atmosphere and Weather
ISBN: 978-0-7166-4276-3 (hc.)

Also available as:
ISBN: 978-0-7166-4286-2 (e-book)

WORLD BOOK STAFF
Executive Committee
President: Geoff Broderick
Vice President, Editorial: Tom Evans
Vice President, Finance: Donald D. Keller
Vice President, Marketing: Jean Lin
Vice President, International: Eddy Kisman
Vice President, Technology: Jason Dole
Director, Human Resources: Bev Ecker

Editorial
Manager, New Content: Jeff De La Rosa
Associate Manager, New Product:
    Nicholas Kilzer
Sr. Editor: Shawn Brennan
Proofreader: Nathalie Strassheim

Graphics and Design
Sr. Visual Communications Designer:
    Melanie Bender
Sr. Web Designer/Digital Media Developer:
    Matt Carrington
Coordinator, Design Development:
    Brenda Tropinski

Acknowledgments:
Writer: Alex Woolf
Illustrator: Steve Evans
Series advisor: Marjorie Frank

Developed with World Book by
White-Thomson Publishing LTD

www.wtpub.co.uk

Additional spot art by Shutterstock

TABLE OF CONTENTS

There is a glossary on page 40. Terms defined in the glossary are in type **that looks like this** on their first appearance.

WHAT IS THE ATMOSPHERE?

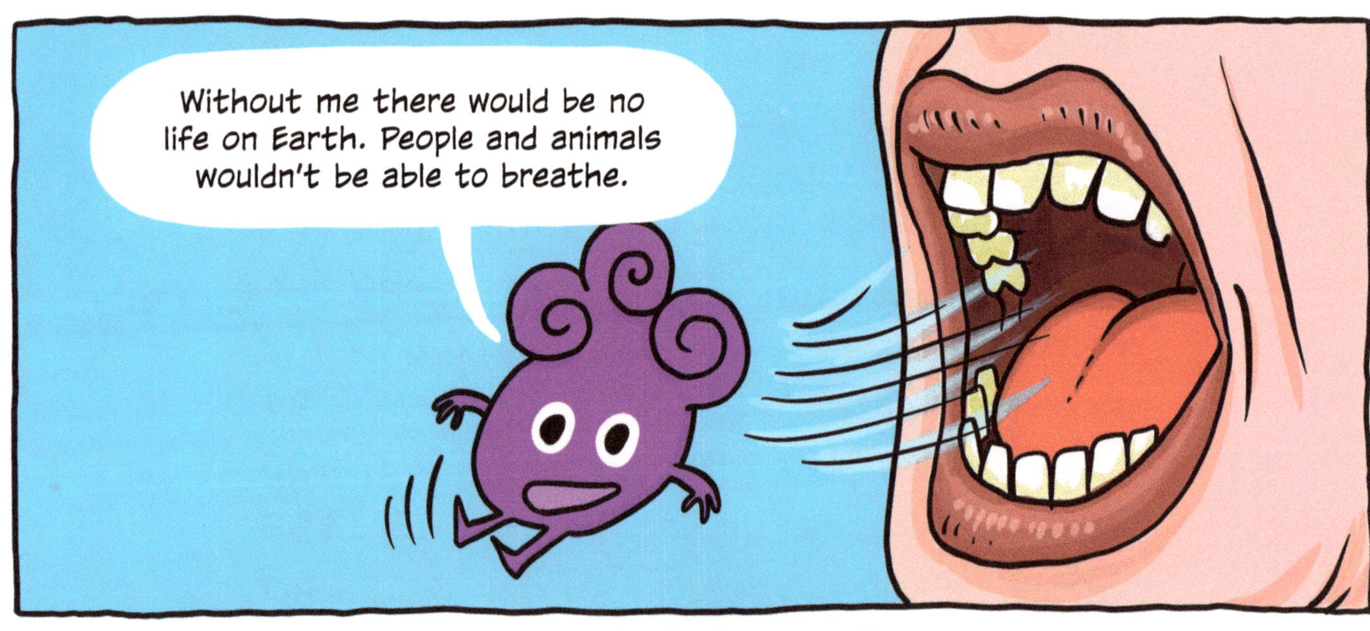

I also absorb harmful **radiation** from the sun.

And the gases I contain, such as carbon dioxide, trap heat from the sun, keeping Earth warm.

Think of me as a life-giving blanket covering our planet. Yet when seen from space, I'm actually quite a thin blanket.

So, it's important to look after me and not pollute me!

I said before that I was a layer of air, but what exactly is air?

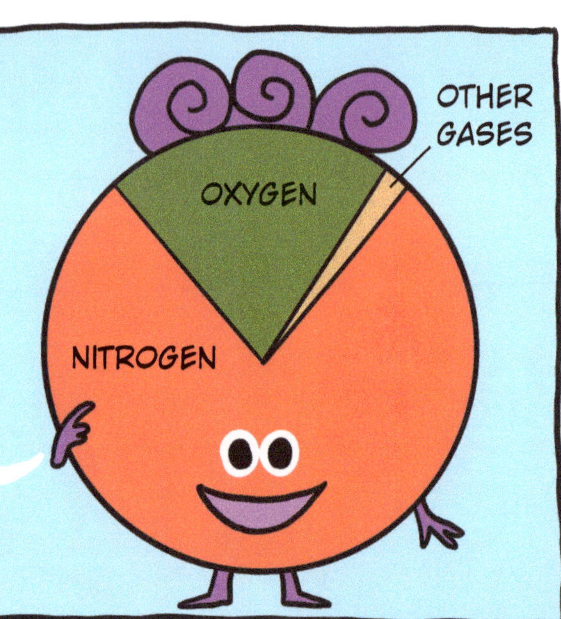

Air is a mixture of gases. Most of it is nitrogen (78 percent) and oxygen (21 percent). The remaining 1 percent is made up of argon, carbon dioxide, and small amounts of other gases.
OTHER GASES
OXYGEN
NITROGEN

The air in the atmosphere gets thinner as you travel farther from Earth's surface.

The air also changes temperature the higher you go. First it gets colder... Brrr!

...and then it gets warmer because of radiation from the sun. Phew!

Hello! I'm Space. I begin where Atmosphere ends.

Scientists have defined the boundary between the atmosphere and space at 62 miles (100 kilometers) above the surface.

Until recently, the only persons who have traveled higher than this have been professional astronauts.
But in 2021, a new era of spaceflight began. And now, some "space tourists" have rocketed beyond Earth's atmosphere.

In fact, there's no definite boundary between the atmosphere and space. I just continue upward, getting thinner and thinner until...

...I eventually fade away.

THE LAYERS OF THE ATMOSPHERE

Height: 50 miles (80 kilometers)

The lowest temperatures in the atmosphere occur in the third layer, the **mesosphere.** Above the poles, summer temperatures can fall below -200 °F (-130 °C). The air in the mesosphere is too thin for airplanes and balloons to fly there.

Height: about 30 miles (48 kilometers)

The second lowest layer, the **stratosphere,** contains around 80 to 90 percent of the atmosphere's ozone (a gas that blocks harmful rays from the sun, protecting life on Earth). The stratosphere is nearly cloudless and extremely dry. In the polar regions, ice clouds form during winter.

Height: about 12 miles (19 kilometers) above the equator and 6 miles (10 kilometers) above the poles.

The uppermost layer, the **thermosphere,** extends all the way into space. The air in the thermosphere is extremely thin and changes in composition the higher you go. Above about 600 miles (1000 kilometers), the thermosphere contains mainly hydrogen and helium.

The lowest layer, the **troposphere,** is where nearly all of Earth's weather happens. Around 80 percent of the atmosphere's mass is in the troposphere. Gases in the troposphere trap some of the sun's heat, keeping Earth warm.

THE WEATHER

Rain, sun, wind, snow. The weather is a constant factor in all our lives.

Fog can make driving difficult.

I can barely see a thing!

Heavy rain can disrupt sports events. Boo!

Weather is the state of the atmosphere at a particular place and time. In this place and time, it's quite windy!

Weather is not the same as climate. Climate is the average weather of a region over a period of time. A region's climate determines whether it looks like this...

Or like this...

Or like this.
So what causes the weather?

The three main factors that control the weather are air temperature...
°C
°F

...air pressure...

...and humidity.
Let's look at each of these in turn...

AIR TEMPERATURE

The air is warmed by radiation arriving from the sun. About 15 percent of the sun's radiation flows back into space, cooling the Earth.

The rest is trapped by gases in the atmosphere and warms Earth. This is called the *greenhouse effect* because the air acts like glass in a greenhouse!

Without the greenhouse effect, the air near Earth's surface would be about 59 °F (33 °C) cooler than it is.

Air temperature also depends on whether it's day or night. The sun's radiation only reaches Earth during daylight hours, so it's colder at night.

And it depends on your **altitude.** Within the troposphere, air temperature drops as you go higher.

Temperature also depends on the season. In winter, the sun is low in the sky and less of its radiation reaches Earth. Days are also shorter, which means fewer hours of sunshine.

The sun's radiation is one way to warm the air. Another way is through **conduction**. To understand that, we first need to learn something about me!

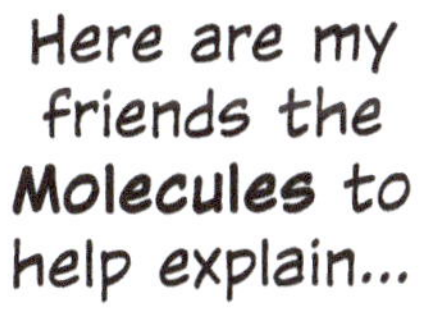

Here are my friends the **Molecules** to help explain...

Heat is a form of energy caused by the motion of molecules (us!) in a substance. If we're not moving around much, the substance will be cold.

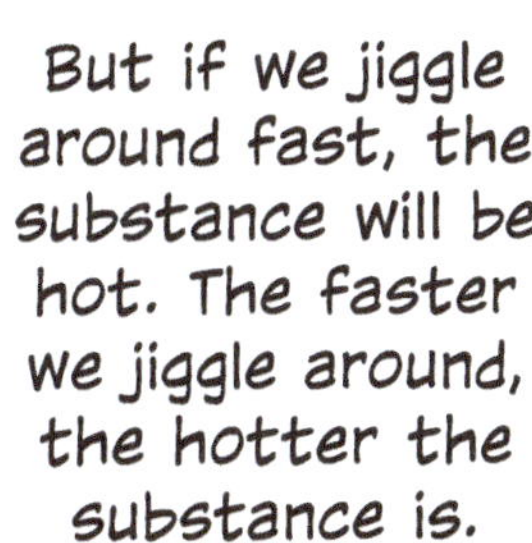

But if we jiggle around fast, the substance will be hot. The faster we jiggle around, the hotter the substance is.

Conduction happens when we bump into each other. This causes heat energy to be transmitted through a substance.

Conduction happens easily in many solids and liquids, where the molecules are closely packed together...

But in the air, molecules are farther apart, so conduction happens more slowly. Even so, conduction does affect the air temperature a little.

During the day, the sun heats the ground by radiation, and the ground in turn heats the air just above it by conduction.

During the night, the air warms the cool ground through conduction.

Remember, conduction is caused by molecules colliding... Ouch!

Convection is a third way air is heated. This is the movement of molecules through a substance... After you, sir!

Conduction happens more easily in a solid because the molecules are tightly packed.

However, convection happens more easily in the air because molecules are free to move about. Wheee!!!!

Convection transfers heat from hot areas to the air. As the air warms, it becomes lighter and rises.

This is my friend Gravity. Gravity keeps you on the ground...

Gravity keeps the air near the ground, too. The weight of the air pressing down on the ground is called air pressure.

You usually can't feel air pressure because your body is built to cope with it.

Air is very light! A bottle of water weighs the same as about 800 bottles of air.

Air pressure changes from place to place. It's lower on a mountain than at sea level because mountains have less air above them.

Air pressure also changes depending on air temperature. Cold air is **dense** with molecules, so it exerts high pressure.
Warm air is less dense, so it exerts low pressure.

Where air pressure is high, you get clear skies.

Where air pressure is low, you get cloudy skies and storms.

A barometer measures air pressure. If it shows it rising, expect fine weather. If it shows it falling, expect rain or snow.
900
1000
1100
1200
1300

Air moves from areas of high pressure, where molecules are squashed together, to areas of low pressure, where molecules are more free to move around. Yay!

This movement of air from high pressure to low pressure is what we call wind. I'll tell you more about wind later!

HUMIDITY

You can't see it, but water is constantly moving through the atmosphere.

The sun's heat turns liquid water into a gas called water vapor. This process is evaporation.

The water vapor rises into the air, then cools and condenses into water droplets to form clouds. This means that the water vapor turns back into a liquid.

When the air can't contain any more water vapor, it is described as saturated.
When the clouds can't hold any more water, the water falls to Earth as rain, sleet, hail, or snow.

This constant movement is called the water cycle.

Humidity is a measure of the amount of water vapor in the air. A hydrometer is an instrument used to measure humidity.

Weather reports often mention relative humidity (RH). This measures how close the air is to being saturated. RH is expressed as a percentage.

So if RH is 100 percent, the air is fully saturated, and the water vapor starts to condense into tiny droplets of water.

When this happens on the ground, we call it fog. If it happens in the sky, we call it a cloud.

Warm air can hold more water vapor than cold air. It takes much less water vapor for cold air to become saturated.

CLOUDS

I love clouds. There are so many different kinds, and they come in such interesting shapes.

They're also useful—bringing water for plants to grow and for us to drink.

All clouds form in the same way: from water vapor rising into the sky by convection.

It's cold up in the sky! Cold air can't hold as much water vapor as warm air, so the air becomes saturated and the water vapor within it condenses into water droplets.

Some of the water droplets cling to microscopic particles in the air and become visible as clouds.

Stratus clouds appear as layers or sheets. These are the low-altitude gray or white clouds you often see on dull, overcast days.

Cumulus clouds appear as rounded masses, piled up on each other. They often remind me of cauliflowers or mashed potato. Yum!

Cirrus clouds are wispy clouds that appear at high altitudes and are formed from ice crystals, not water droplets. They remind me of tufts of hair. How do I look?

Say hello to my friend Wind. He seems friendly now, but he can be quite moody.

Sometimes he can be a gentle breeze...

At other times, he's a violent blast that can cause serious damage.

I can change the weather by carrying cool air to warm places.

I can whip up giant waves that capsize boats and flood the land...

Or I can blow clouds away to reveal the sunshine.

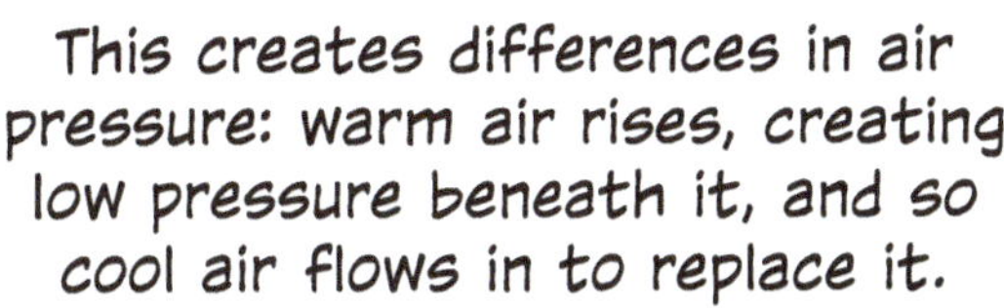

Wind happens because the sun doesn't heat Earth evenly. There are areas of warm air and areas of cool air...

This creates differences in air pressure: warm air rises, creating low pressure beneath it, and so cool air flows in to replace it.

The sun heats the land more quickly than it does the sea. Air warmed by the land rises, causing cooler sea air to flow in.

Other winds happen because of effects that occur over large areas of the Earth's surface. These are called prevailing winds.

PREVAILING WINDS
Prevailing winds are giant belts of wind that continually circle our planet.
We have these winds because the sun heats Earth's surface unevenly. It shines directly on the areas at the equator and at an angle on areas farther north or south.

As a result, places near the equator are warmer and the air pressure is low. Hey, I feel so relaxed!
EQUATOR

It's colder at the poles, which means air pressure is higher here.
NORTH POLE

Cool, high-pressure air from the poles moves toward the equator.
At the equator, it pushes up the warm air, which flows back toward the poles, and so on, in a continuous cycle.

Because Earth rotates, the winds blow in a curve rather than a straight line toward the equator. This is called the **Coriolis effect**.

In the Northern Hemisphere, winds curve to the right... In the Southern Hemisphere, they curve to the left.

The Coriolis effect also causes winds near Earth's surface to split into three belts of winds in each hemisphere - trade winds, westerlies, and polar easterlies.

These winds always blow from the same direction and have a big effect on the weather. For instance, the trade winds create a band of rainy weather near the equator.

Come on, blow—will you! Between the belts of strong winds are zones of very little wind. These are called the Horse Latitudes and the Doldrums.

AIR MASSES
An air mass is a huge volume of air that has roughly the same temperature and humidity throughout.
And when I say huge, I mean HUGE! An air mass covers thousands of miles or kilometers!

An air mass can form whenever the atmosphere stays in contact with a large area of land or sea for a long time. Mind if I hang around?

Air masses that form over land are dry. Air masses that form over water are humid.

An air mass that develops in the Arctic will be cold. Brrr!

An air mass that develops near the equator will be warm. Mmmm! This is nice!

The four basic types of air mass are cold and dry, cold and humid, warm and dry, and warm and humid.

When winds move air masses, the air masses carry their weather with them. Hello, warm, dry land! I'm cold and wet!

As an air mass moves, its temperature and humidity can change as it moves over land or water. Hey, I'm feeling warmer and drier!

If a warm, humid air mass is forced up a mountain, its temperature drops and the relative humidity rises, leading to rain. Sorry! Blame the mountain!

Help! We're going to crash!
Where air masses meet,
it's called a front.
WARM AIR
COLD AIR

Up we go! When an advancing warm air
mass meets a retreating cold air mass,
the warm air rises, being less dense.
This is called a warm front.
WARM AIR
COLD AIR

Going under! When an advancing cold air mass
meets a retreating warm air mass, the cold
air, being more dense, moves under the warm
air, pushing it up. This is a cold front.
WARM AIR
COLD AIR

In both warm and cold fronts, when the warm air rises, the temperature drops and the relative humidity rises. The result is therefore often clouds and rain.

Cold Front is catching up! Cold fronts move faster than warm fronts. So cold fronts often catch up with warm fronts and merge with them.
COLD AIR
WARM AIR
When fronts merge, they become one front, called an occluded front. It has the characteristics of both a warm and cold front.

COLD AIR
WARM AIR
COOL AIR
Where are you, Warm Air? Occluded means "hidden." In an occluded front the warm air is lifted from the surface and therefore hidden from view.

EXTREME WEATHER

A blizzard is an intense snowstorm with high winds and freezing temperatures. Yoo-hoo! I'm over here!
Blizzards happen at cold fronts—when a very cold air mass from the poles runs into a warm, humid air mass. The warm air mass cools as it is pushed up and its moisture falls as snow—lots of it!
Hurricanes are powerful storms with violent winds that can reach up to 200 miles (320 kilometers) per hour. That's extremely fast!
Hurricanes develop over warm, tropical ocean waters. Warm, moist air rises, creating an area of low pressure beneath. Air rushes in and starts to swirl around a still, central area—the eye of the storm.

A tornado is a rapidly spinning column of air that has reached the ground. It's the most violent of all storms.
Hey, I'm getting dizzy!
STORM CHASER

LOOKING AFTER THE ATMOSPHERE

The **ozone layer** in the stratosphere helps block dangerous radiation from the sun. Good work, Ozone!

But oh no! I see a hole! Chemicals called chlorofluorocarbons (CFC's) destroy ozone molecules.
CFC's are found in aerosol sprays, refrigerators, air conditioners, and other products.

Good news! Since the late 1980's, countries have been phasing out the production and use of CFC's, and now the ozone is recovering.

We can all help protect the atmosphere by cutting down on car journeys and walking or cycling to school. Hey, this is fun!

We can also plant more trees and plants. They absorb CO_2 and help clean the air!

Thanks for doing your bit to protect the atmosphere!

ACTIVITY: WEATHER OR NOT!

All the weather forecasters on television or radio have an annoying habit of talking about the weather without saying exactly what it is! See if you can give the correct term for the weather condition or event that they describe.

1. "These will make for a dull, overcast day all around!" _______

2. "The weather tonight will be dominated by air movement that is caused by air moving from areas of high to low pressure." _______

3. "We'll be surrounded for a few days with lighter air that rises." _______

4. "Residents will need to evacuate due to a storm with extremely high winds developing offshore, over the warm tropical ocean." _______

5. "These wispy clouds signal a change in the weather is coming!" _______

6. "Get ready for a weekend of high winds and heavy, blowing snow." _______

See page 40 for answers.

WORDS TO KNOW

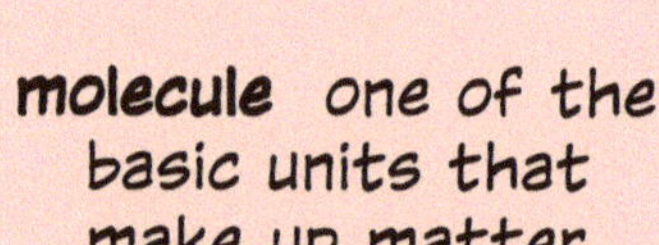

air mass a large body of air with about the same temperature, humidity, and pressure throughout.

air pressure the weight of air pressing down on Earth.

altitude the height of an object above Earth's surface.

cold front the boundary where an advancing cold air mass meets a retreating warm air mass.

conduction the process by which heat energy is transmitted through the collision of molecules within a substance.

convection the process by which heat energy is transmitted through the movement of molecules through a substance.

Coriolis effect an effect caused by the rotation of Earth, deflecting winds and causing them to move in a curve.

dense tightly packed.

evaporation the process by which a liquid turns into vapor.

global warming a gradual increase in the overall temperature of Earth's atmosphere.

greenhouse gas any gas that contributes to the greenhouse effect by trapping more of the sun's heat in the atmosphere.

mesosphere the region of Earth's atmosphere above the stratosphere and below the thermosphere.

molecule one of the basic units that make up matter.

ozone layer a layer in the stratosphere that contains a high concentration of the gas ozone.

radiation energy that travels from a heat source in the form of waves or energized particles.

saturation a state in which something is so soaked with water that no more can be absorbed.

stratosphere the region of Earth's atmosphere above the troposphere and below the mesosphere.

thermosphere the topmost layer of the atmosphere.

troposphere the lowest layer of the atmosphere.

warm front the boundary where an advancing warm air mass meets a retreating cold air mass.

water vapor water in the form of tiny droplets suspended in the air.

ACTIVITY ANSWERS 1. Stratus clouds; 2. Wind; 3. Low pressure; 4. Hurricane; 5. Cirrus clouds; 6. Blizzard; 7. Humidity; 8. Cumulus clouds; 9. Tornado; 10. High pressure; 11. Temperature; 12. Front